IMAGES
of America
TUZIGOOT NATIONAL MONUMENT

This sign at the main entry gate to Tuzigoot greets visitors every day. It is interesting to note the modern abstract representation of the ancient stone pueblo nearly 80 years after the National Park Service took over stewardship of the site and over 900 years after construction of the complex was started. (Author's collection.)

ON THE COVER: This 1934 photograph shows workmen excavating the rooms of the Tuzigoot pueblo. The laborer in the foreground uses a pick to break up hard-packed dirt before shovels, then later trowels and brushes, were used to locate, uncover, and catalog any artifacts that remained. Centuries of accumulated debris was removed down to the original floor level. (Courtesy National Park Service.)

IMAGES
of America

TUZIGOOT NATIONAL MONUMENT

Rod Timanus

ARCADIA
PUBLISHING

Copyright © 2017 by Rod Timanus
ISBN 978-1-4671-2486-7

Published by Arcadia Publishing
Charleston, South Carolina

Printed in the United States of America

Library of Congress Control Number: 2016911767

For all general information, please contact Arcadia Publishing:
Telephone 843-853-2070
Fax 843-853-0044
E-mail sales@arcadiapublishing.com
For customer service and orders:
Toll-Free 1-888-313-2665

Visit us on the Internet at www.arcadiapublishing.com

On the occasion of the National Park Service's 100th birthday in 2016, this book is gratefully dedicated to all the selfless rangers, staff, and volunteers, past and present, who protect and maintain this marvelous window on the past.

Contents

Acknowledgments — 6
Introduction — 7
1.   The People — 13
2.   The Place — 21
3.   Uncovering the Past — 27
Bibliography — 95

Acknowledgments

Writing is a singular occupation; only you can put the words on the paper. But getting the information and images you need to create those words properly and then getting them to the printed page is a joint effort. I have been aided in this effort by many talented people and offer my gratitude for their contributions to this work.

Initially, I must thank the staff and rangers at Montezuma Castle National Monument for encouraging me to write this book about Tuzigoot, especially Mindi Gusman, the park store manager at both Montezuma Castle and Tuzigoot National Monuments. Park archeologists Matt Guebard and Lucas Hoedl aided in my exploration of the photograph archives housed in the ranger offices at the Tuzigoot location. Meghann M. Vance, coprincipal investigator at the Anthropology Laboratories of Northern Arizona University tracked down many photograph captions from the 1940s for me that I was beginning to think were lost forever. Caitrin Cunningham, title manager at Arcadia Publishing, ushered me through the process of getting my words into print. Lastly, Barbara Prichard graciously photographed areas of the site for me for inclusion in this book. Other talented photographers also contributed images and are given credit where their work appears. Unless otherwise noted, all photographs are courtesy of the National Park Service.

I am grateful to all of them and hope the reader will appreciate their efforts as much as I do.

Introduction

Twelve million years ago, the Verde Valley of Arizona was a vast, shallow inland lake, 15 miles wide and nearly 30 miles long. The cataclysmic collapse of a volcanically formed lava dam at one end may have caused the water to flow out or natural evaporation may have occurred during prolonged dry periods, leaving behind a steep-sided, cave-pocked valley still being fed by the underground springs that had once filled the lake and the meandering Verde River.

When the people known today as the Sinagua arrived centuries later, they borrowed heavily from the knowledge of surrounding tribal groups known as the Anasazi and Hohokam for techniques of building and farming. Eventually, as humans always do, they banded together to form large cooperative communities. Throughout the valley, they cleared the land, dug irrigation canals, planted various crops, hunted, and built structures. By most estimates, there are nearly 400 identified Sinagua building sites in the Verde Valley, located approximately two miles apart and ranging in size from one- and two-room structures to complexes of 20 rooms or more. How many caves were inhabited at one time or another cannot be estimated.

We call them the Sinagua. That title is derived from the name the Spanish used to describe the northern San Francisco Peaks area near present-day Flagstaff, Arizona, in which the original group lived, Sierra de Sin Agua, or "mountains without water." In the 1930s, the name Sinagua was applied to the entire group and continues to this day, even though the region the Southern branch lived in was far from arid. There are two distinct branches of the Sinagua people, Northern and Southern. The Southern Sinagua migrated south into the fertile, well-watered Verde Valley around AD 700.

They were primitive farmers, hunters, builders, craftsmen, and traders. They flourished in their home territory for nearly 800 years before they simply packed up and moved away. They left behind no written or spoken language and no evidence of their spiritual beliefs—not even the name they called themselves. What they left, however, was a series of structures built from surrounding native materials that would define them as a people to future archeologists and historians.

It is the stone structures they erected that denote their passing. What the Sinagua left behind is truly unique in the fact that everything they built was constructed of the natural materials at hand using primitive stone tools and the power of their intellect and muscle alone. What survived into the modern age as curious ruins is an indelible footprint left by a people who no longer exist but are still alive in the mind and imagination.

The place now known as Tuzigoot is just one such footprint. Over the span of 400 years, beginning around AD 1000, the stone and mud pueblo grew and expanded up, down, and atop a prominent ridge rising 120 feet above the middle Verde Valley floor. It eventually grew to contain nearly 90 rooms, capable of housing several hundred people. Many were two-story structures, and all were accessed through an entryway located in the roof, necessitating the use of ladders to enter and exit the building. There is no evidence that they were warlike in nature, although the crumbling remains of their community pueblos, Tuzigoot especially, were later often mistaken for fortresses. There is plentiful evidence, however, to indicate that they were willing trade partners with neighboring groups far and wide.

At the pueblo, the seasons changed, bringing a variety of new and familiar daily activities, and the years passed quietly. The pueblo brimmed with life, young and old working side by side in a harmony of common goals and purpose. They knew there was a world outside their own, goods were bartered and traded with people from far away locales, but they seemed content where they were. Then, around the year 1400, the situation unexplainably changed.

The Sinagua people of the Verde Valley simply began to leave their home territory for no as yet discovered reason, abandoning all they had worked so long and mightily to build and maintain. By 1425, the pueblo was totally empty and devoid of life, a shell that the human spirit had gone out of. Within 100 years, the pueblo fell into disrepair and began to crumble down upon itself, leaving only oddly configured piles of stones to mark its location.

Seasons continued to change, and years continued to pass quietly, but the remains of the pueblo stood silent and lifeless. Nomadic native people, the Apache and the Yavapai, moved about the Verde Valley, but neither utilized nor took much notice of the structures the long-departed Sinagua had left behind. In 1583, a new race of men, the Spanish, rode through the Verde Valley on their way to seek out fabled riches rumored to lie nearby. Even though they must have passed within sight of the abandoned pueblo, their journals chronicling the trip contain no mention of it.

In the centuries to follow, several countries claimed ownership of the land that encompassed the area once occupied by the Sinagua people. Initially, in the 1500s and 1600s, the Spanish claimed the area by right of conquest over the native peoples of the American Southwest. In 1821, it became the possession of Mexico after a successful revolution there expelled the Spanish. Then, in 1848, the land was handed over to the United States as part of the peace settlement at the end of the war with Mexico. In 1863, during the American Civil War, the territory of Arizona was created by an act of Congress and signed into law by Pres. Abraham Lincoln. Throughout all this changing of ownership, the ruins of the pueblo on the hill stood silent and unnoticed. American settlers, farmers, ranchers, and miners began to occupy the area after the Civil War. Ongoing conflicts between the newcomers and the native peoples soon brought the US Army.

It would not be until Dr. Edgar A. Mearns, an Army surgeon stationed at Fort Verde in Arizona Territory from 1884 to 1888, began his systematic study of the ancient sites in the Verde Valley that the pueblo was brought to light. Though he was primarily concerned with the more visible Montezuma Castle cliff site just over 20 miles away, Means did explore and make brief notes about the hilltop pueblo. In an article published later in an 1890 issue of the *Popular Science Monthly*, he warns that the overdevelopment of the Verde Valley is putting the ancient ruins there at risk of destruction. He had good reason to be concerned.

By 1879, the agricultural town of Cottonwood had already been established south and west of the pueblo site. Cottonwood supplied foodstuffs and goods to not only the soldiers at Fort Verde, but also to the copper miners in Jerome. Large tracts of land had been cleared and the Verde River diverted in several places to irrigate the fields of crops, with no attention being paid to what ancient sites might have been destroyed in the process. As early as 1888, the United Verde Copper Company, under the direction of industrialist William Clark, was operating mines and smelters in Jerome, within distant sight of the pueblo, and laying down railroad tracks to transport the processed copper bars out of the valley.

In the decades to follow, and into the early part of the 20th century, the copper mining industry and cattle ranching grew and expanded in the middle Verde Valley. The tall smokestacks of copper ore smelters in Cottonwood and the mine workers town of Clarkdale belched smoke and toxic fumes into the air, killing off nearby vegetation, and the waste by-product of the smelting process, called tailings, was pumped onto the low-lying valley floor. The wet slurry deposited there dried to a fine orange-yellowish powder that every hint of a breeze picked up and swirled about; clouds of the stuff settled on and coated everything in the vicinity, including the buried ruins of the hilltop pueblo.

By that time the location of the pueblo was known to the local population, efforts were already under way to protect and preserve the ancient Sinagua ruins that remained throughout the entire Verde Valley. In 1932, a survey crew mapped the pueblo site in preparation for a more thorough investigation. Under the auspices of the Yavapi County Chamber of Commerce Archaeological Committee and the Arizona State Museum, two graduate archeology students at the University of Arizona, Louis Caywood and Edward Spicer, were commissioned to undertake an excavation and preservation project at the site in 1933. Any artifacts discovered were to go to a small museum located in Prescott after being cleaned and repaired. The United Verde Copper Company, owners of the property where the pueblo was located, granted permission for the site excavation.

The excavation began with a crew of eight local men, but when the project received funding from the federal Civil Works Administration, a government agency in charge of creating jobs during the Great Depression of the 1930s, the workforce grew to 48 laborers. Most of the men were unemployed copper mine workers and were no strangers to the backbreaking toil of moving earth and rock. They did, however, have to be schooled in the delicate work of uncovering, protecting, and removing fragile artifacts. For eight months, the men worked on the site, removing debris, stabilizing wall foundations, and cataloging and removing artifacts.

By June 1934, the project was complete and the pueblo was named Tuzigoot. Caywood and Spicer published their report on the site work in 1935, and the next year a small museum was built that still serves as the Visitor Center today. In 1937, the superintendent of the Southwestern National Monuments, Frank Pinkley, lobbied to have the site included in the National Park Service's growing list of holdings. The United Verde Copper Company sold the site to Yavapai County for the sum of $1 in 1939, and the county immediately turned it over to the federal government. Pres. Franklin Roosevelt designated Tuzigoot, and 43 acres of land surrounding it, a national monument open to the public in July 1939.

The trip to Tuzigoot was not easy for the first visitors, so far off the beaten path was the location, but the people did come. They had to brave the choking clouds of copper tailings dust that still remained on the valley floor long after copper mining and smelting ceased in the early 1950s; a thorough cleanup of the area was completed in 2006. The acres of tailings were first covered with two feet of trucked-in dirt, the land was graded to facilitate proper drainage to the Verde River through underground rock channels built for that purpose, and the entire area was reseeded with native vegetation. No evidence of the previous environmental disaster remains today, and visitors see surrounding scenery very much like that the ancient Sinagua might have gazed upon.

The abandoned old pueblo once again feels the tread of human feet and hears the voices of young and old ringing throughout the remains of the dwellings. People returned to Tuzigoot after so many centuries of silence, and the spirit of the place returned with them.

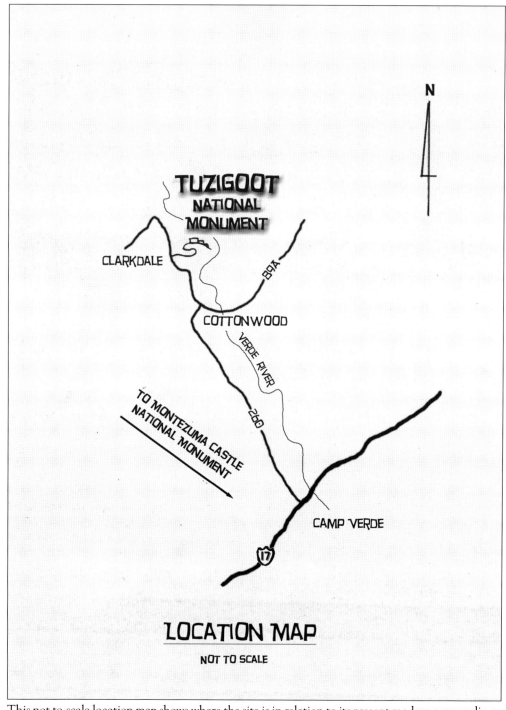

This not-to-scale location map shows where the site is in relation to its present modern surroundings. Although the towns of Cottonwood, Clarkdale, and nearby Jerome are popular tourist destinations accessed from Route 89A, finding Tuzigoot is not easy for some. But it is well worth the effort to do so. Its remote location only heightens the sense of visiting an ancient time and place. (Author's collection.)

The earliest known photograph of what was later named Tuzigoot Hill, seen in the background, was taken around 1918 by Arthur J. Faul, who lived on a ranch to the southwest of the site from 1917 to 1921. It would be 15 years before an excavation crew would climb to the top of the ridge and begin to uncover the ancient pueblo that lay beneath the rubble. Faul was obviously very proud of his flock of chickens, as they are featured prominently in the foreground of his shot.

Pictured is a view of the west side of the complex from below. This is the sight that today greets visitors driving up the main road to the Visitor Center to begin their journey of exploration into the distant past. (Courtesy Barbara Prichard.)

A pre-1933 view of the unexcavated hilltop is seen here. Nature had reclaimed the area and hidden all traces of the old pueblo. The location of the site was known only to some local residents, a few archeologists, and the pothunters who had scavenged the pueblo for artifacts to sell.

This view shows the unexcavated site before 1933. It is amazing to consider that there is a human dwelling site beneath all the underbrush and rubble seen in this photograph. Unless one was looking for it, one would never know it was even there.

One

The People

Today, they would be considered a very primitive people, but the ancient Sinagua were quite innovative and industrious for their time and place in history.

Typically, the men stood barely five feet, four inches tall on average and were of a thin, yet muscular, physique that befitted their lifestyle of daily hard work. The women were just five feet in height but were as hardy as their men. Their wardrobe consisted of woven cotton fabric that varied with the seasons, loincloths for the men and plain skirts or off-the-shoulder shifts for the women. On their feet, they wore sandals woven from yucca leaves. Their lives revolved around the changing seasons, planting, harvesting, and hunting. The surrounding landscape provided them with everything they needed to survive and prosper. On the broad floodplains of the Verde Valley, they grew a variety of crops that included corn, squash, beans, and cotton. They dug irrigation ditches to water their fields from nearby rivers and streams. They domesticated dogs and turkeys; hunted deer, rabbits, and waterfowl; and used native plants as food, medicines, dyes, and items of apparel.

They were also prolific builders. Using only rudimentary stone tools and the strength of their muscles alone, they raised wood and stone structures that would stand for centuries after their passing. Their strong sense of community brought them together to dwell in large numbers, and their sense of place in the larger world made them willing trade partners with other native groups far and wide. Some artifacts uncovered at their dwelling sites are items not of their making or native to their environment.

If they were spiritual in their beliefs, there is no real hard evidence of it. They did create pictographs, or rock art paintings, the meanings of which are not known. It does not appear that they were interested in adorning their dwellings or pottery with symbols. But there is a Verde Valley location today known as Palatki Ruins, near present-day Sedona, Arizona, where their rock art appears in abundance. This could indicate that there was some significance to that site for the Sinagua people who lived nearby—just one more mystery left behind for us to ponder by a vanished race of people.

A Sinagua man is carrying a load of stones up the hill for use in constructing rooms in the pueblo. Bundles of sticks, branches, and small tree trunks would follow, as would dirt and water to make the mud mortar to hold the construction together. All building materials were moved and assembled by hand. (Author's collection.)

In a newly constructed room still devoid of many household conveniences such as a firepit and other everyday items, a Sinagua woman is repairing some of her weaving. Stone and mud are natural insulators, keeping the dwelling cool in the summer and warm in the winter. (Author's collection.)

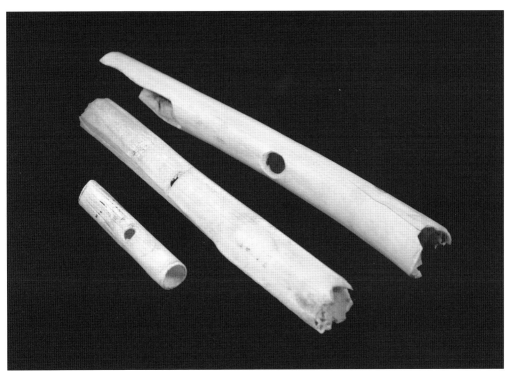

A trio of excavated bird bone whistles is pictured here—hawk bones on both sides and a turkey bone in the middle. The Sinagua hunted hawks and domesticated turkeys. Their hardscrabble existence was obviously eased a bit by being able to create musical tones on these instruments during rare moments of relaxation.

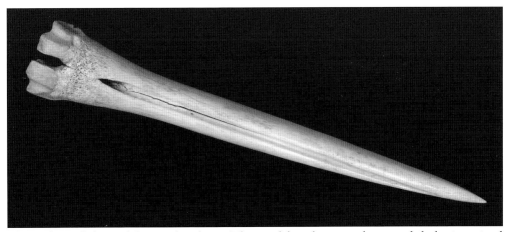

This awl was fashioned from a deer bone. This useful tool was used to punch holes in animal skins and woven fabrics. It could also be used for sewing stitches. To supplement their agricultural efforts, the Sinagua hunted and fished the surrounding woods and streams. Almost nothing usable from an animal or fish carcass went to waste.

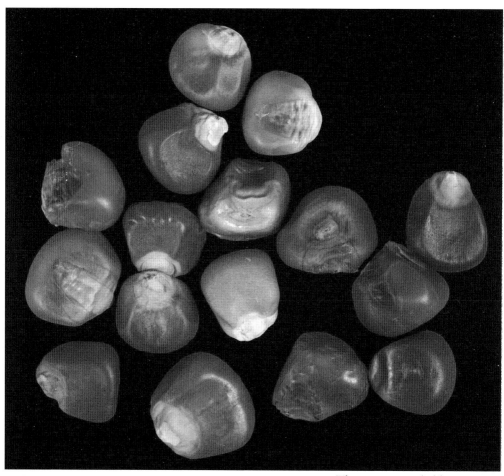

These are remarkably preserved ancient kernels of corn. Corn was the primary food staple of the Sinagua and was cultivated on the flatlands below the pueblo, as well as close to all their dwelling sites throughout the Verde Valley.

These charred beans were removed from an excavated firepit on site. Along with corn, beans were also an important food staple grown by the Sinagua in their fields nearby. The Sinagua supplemented the vegetables and legumes in their diets with local berries when they were in season.

This is a necklace made of stone beads. Whether they were decorative, ceremonial, or used as a trade item is unknown. But this excavated item does indicate that there was a certain amount of leisure time to spend just being artistic and creative.

Quids of chewed yucca leaves are seen here. Chewing the leaves was to either soften the fibers to make them pliable for weaving and sewing, or for the juices as possibly a mild stimulant. The intact leaves were also used to weave mats and sandals.

This whimsical frog pendant was carved from a seashell. Since there was no ocean nearby, it is evidence that the Sinagua were part of a vast native trade network that bartered goods back and forth over great distances. The trade network stretched to the Pacific Ocean to the west and ancient Mexico to the south and included many different tribal groups. As further proof, the mummified remains of a parrot indigenous to present-day northern Mexico were also found at the site.

In the 1934 excavation, plain pottery was uncovered where it had remained buried under rubble for centuries. This pot is incredibly undamaged and was returned to its original location for this photograph. Most clay pots of this type were found cracked or broken into pieces.

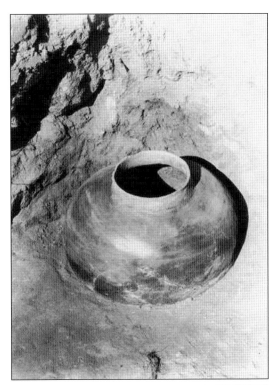

Examples of repaired Sinagua pots that were excavated from the site in 1934 are on display today in the Visitor Center. All the artifacts were cleaned and cataloged, and many were glued back together by volunteers working at a nearby Clarkdale public school during the excavation. (Courtesy Barbara Prichard.)

A row of metates and grinding stones, or manos, is displayed in one of the rooms. A few were left in the complex, while most of the others were relocated for museum displays. These items were usually left behind when a Sinagua family relocated, as they were too heavy to carry and were easily replaced. (Courtesy David Rose, www.arizonaruins.com.)

A metate is on display in one of the rooms. The chipped corner indicates that even stone implements could be damaged when a wall collapsed centuries ago. Because of the large former population of the pueblo, Tuzigoot has the largest collection of these artifacts in the region. (Courtesy Barbara Prichard.)

Two

The Place

The pueblo is now called Tuzigoot. It is not a word from the Sinagua language; nobody knows what that language sounded like. In fact, because of a misinterpretation of sound and spelling, the name Tuzigoot is not from any language at all.

Near the completion of the 1933–1934 excavation and restoration of the site, archeologists Caywood and Spicer needed a name for the location and solicited ideas from members of the work crew. It was workman Ben Lewis, of Tonto Apache heritage, who suggested the Apache name Tu' zighoot (pronounced Two-see-Whoodt). The name translates to "Crooked Water," and it was descriptive of the nearby Verde River and Peck's Lake that were visible from the hilltop pueblo. The archeologists liked the name, but mistakenly spelled it, as it sounded to them, Tuzigoot (pronounced Two-zee-goot) in their subsequent published report on the project. "Tuzigoot" has absolutely no meaning in the Apache language.

The pueblo (Tuzigoot) was located atop a nearly flat-topped ridge of limestone that rose 120 to 150 feet above the valley floor and overlooked a tree-lined watercourse (the Verde River), a spring-fed marsh (Tavasci Marsh), and a lake (Peck's Lake). The complex itself was built in stages, not as a single unit, with each cluster of new construction sprawling out over the top and sides of the ridge as natural contours allowed. Over four centuries, beginning around AD 1000, rooms were added, rebuilt, or abandoned depending on the needs of the populace. In many rooms, a second, or perhaps even a third, floor was built on an existing structure when outward expansion proved too difficult because of the sloping terrain. The Sinagua building technique at the pueblo was simple yet strong and lasting. Unshaped stones were just piled up atop each other and held in place with mud mortar to create walls. Cottonwood, juniper, and sycamore trees provided roof beams, support posts, and entry ladders. All building materials had to be hauled up the ridge by hand. In addition to this backbreaking toil, as the population grew, more irrigation canals had to be dug to bring water from the river to the ever-expanding cleared and cultivated fields in the valley below.

For over 400 years, the Sinagua worked and thrived in their fertile environment. Then they simply packed up and left it all behind.

1100s

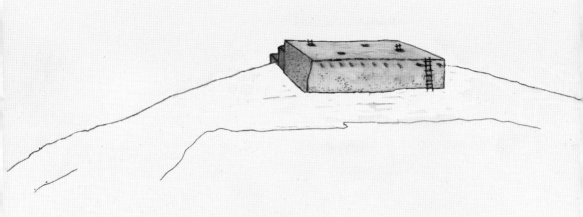

12 Rooms

Pictured is an artist's conception of the early stages of the pueblo development. (Author's collection.)

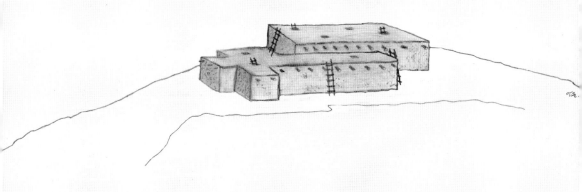

This artist's conception shows the continuing development of the pueblo as more and more people gathered at the site. (Author's collection.)

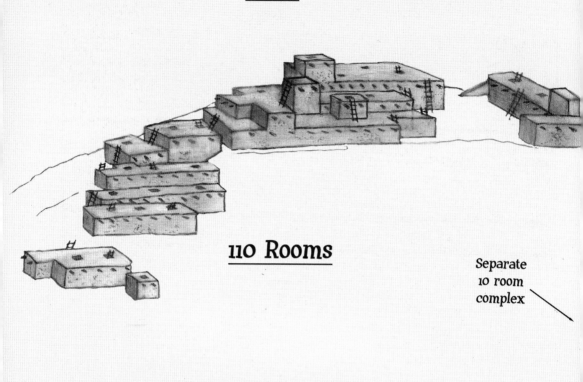

An artist's conception of the final configuration of the pueblo before it was abandoned is seen here. (Author's collection.)

This glass-enclosed diorama of the Tuzigoot pueblo is displayed in the Visitor Center and presents an aerial view of what the pueblo may have looked like when it was originally occupied. Its origin is unknown, but it may have been created by John L. Cotter, the first National Park Service director of Tuzigoot National Monument. (Author's collection.)

A photographic abstract view of the Tuzigoot diorama from the side is shown here. This scene could very well be considered a view of the pueblo as the sun rises behind it and may be a more realistic depiction in that respect. (Courtesy Barbara Prichard.)

This was the sight that greeted the 1934 excavation crew. The hilltop was overrun by centuries of accumulated vegetation and rubble. The task of excavation ahead must have seemed daunting at the time, but the crew members were undeterred and would finish the task in just about a year and a half.

In this 1935 photograph taken from the west, the Tuzigoot pueblo is barely visible atop the first ridge above the line of trees in the center of the shot. Since the complex was built of all-natural materials and blends in with its surroundings, one has to look closely to see the dark squares of the rooms, a shape that does not occur in nature but is man-made (see insert). In the foreground is the Verde River, while a motor vehicle, light reflecting off its top, can be seen above and paralleling the river driving away from the site on the dirt access road. This view would have been very much like what would have been seen when the pueblo was complete and occupied over six centuries ago.

Three

Uncovering the Past

When Caywood, Spicer, and their crew began the site excavation, they started with the archeologist's equivalent of "Dumpster diving."

Over the centuries of habitation, the Sinagua had simply thrown their household refuse and human waste off the side of the ridge in the same locations on the northeast and northwest sides. In time, the decomposing garbage accumulated to depths of from 7 to 11 feet or more. Previous pothunters dug into these midden deposits seeking artifacts, leaving animal and human bone fragments, along with potsherds and other implements strewn about. Seeking evidence of everyday life and diet, the crew trenched diagonally across the deposits, from the bottoms of the slopes toward the tops, at three-foot intervals and verified that the Sinagua had actually buried their adult dead in the soft compost rather than struggle with digging graves in the nearly solid rock of the ridge. On the west slope, near the summit, the crew was surprised to find the remains of a series of rooms that had been abandoned and buried beneath the refuse.

In the next phase of the work, the remains of the pueblo were divided into numbered sections of rooms, designated as groups with numbered rooms and dug out. The remains of many children were discovered buried in the floors of the rooms once excavation reached the original floor level. They were reinterred where they were found after the room was cleared. During excavation, it was evident that the stones used in the walls of the rooms were not shaped to fit tightly with each other but were laid out in their original form and mortared in with mud. A coating of that same mud was thickly applied inside and out to create a semi-smooth wall surface. Since no exterior doorways were found, all indications were that entry to the rooms was through a hole in the roof via ladders.

Stabilizing the walls that were still standing, up to the point of their collapse, with modern concrete would later create problems with moisture retention and drainage that needed to be redone later with a more authentic mixture of mud and mortar. That mixture is still used for maintenance work. Many excavated wall stones not utilized in reconstruction were used to build the small museum, later a Visitor Center, to the north of the pueblo.

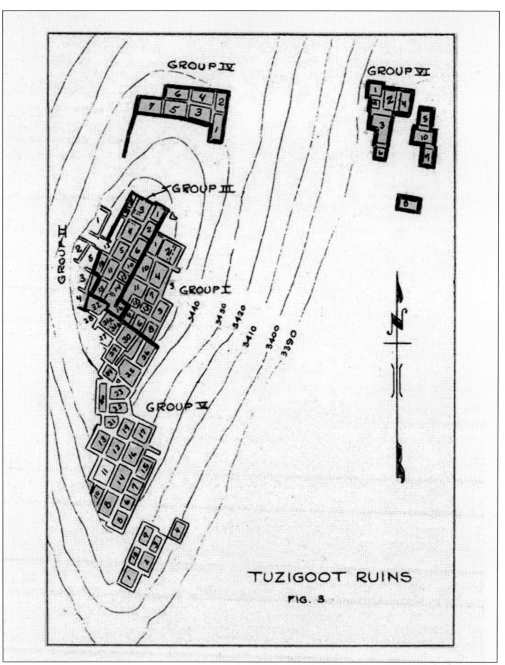

This location map appears in the 1935 report *Tuzigoot: The Excavation and Repair of a Ruin on the Verde River near Clarkdale, Arizona*, by Louis R. Caywood and Edward H. Spicer, printed by the National Park Service Field Division of Education. Although the site was not uncovered in the sequence it is numbered here, it remains the most extensively excavated and partially restored Sinagua site in the Verde Valley of Arizona. Montezuma Castle, also a national monument administered by the National Park Service, some 20 miles away in the town of Camp Verde, was discovered largely intact and more protected from the elements beneath a cliff overhang than was the hilltop Tuzigoot.

The excavation crew is working on a shed to house a power generator so that electricity could be brought in to illuminate the worksite. Power poles have already been put up but lack any wiring. A toolshed would also be erected close by.

After excavation began, stones that could be reused for any reconstruction work were neatly stacked up near the working area. In this photograph, they are seen close to some uncovered walls. Note the old and new forms of transportation in the background—a horse and several motor vehicles.

This 1934 photograph shows the hillside at the start of the excavation. The excavation crew faced a daunting task, and the labor would be backbreaking. But the end result of the work would long endure as a window to the past and a vanished people.

This 1934 photograph was taken at the top of the hill and shows the remains of room walls beginning to be uncovered, after several centuries of being hidden from sight, with the removal of the underbrush concealing the site.

This 1934 photograph was shot looking up from below. All the underbrush has been removed from the hilltop work area, and the next phase of the work, the excavation of the pueblo walls and rooms, has started. Stabilization and partial reconstruction of a few sections would follow.

A workman carefully shovels away loose dirt and debris down to the original hard-packed floor. This slow and tedious work was performed in every room of the pueblo so as not to disturb or damage any artifacts that rested below the rubble.

A workman stopped long enough to pose for this 1934 photograph. The nearby towns of Jerome (established in 1876), Cottonwood (established in 1879), and Clarkdale (established in 1912) were still small and sparsely populated at this time, contributing to the feeling of isolation at the pueblo worksite.

Crew members are on the hillside, carefully removing accumulated soil. Note the metate and grinding stone, or mono, resting where they were placed after excavation and location documentation, to the right of the crouching workman. The remains of a support pole are visible just in front of the workman's leg.

Here is another 1934 posed shot of a workman amid the fruits of his labor. The remains of a wall are visible beside him. Just as the Sinagua had used only the strength of their muscles to build the pueblo, so too did the excavation crew members, armed with picks and shovels, use theirs to uncover the ancient ruins hundreds of years later.

This photograph shows a supervisor making notes on the condition of the site and the progress of excavation being made. Each stage of the work was fully documented and photographed, then later turned into a concise report on the overall project.

The crew is working atop the complex. In the foreground, just left of center in the bottom of the photograph, is a room yet to be cleared of debris from a collapsed wall. In the distance below, in the direction of the town of Cottonwood to the south, is the Verde River.

The crew is clearing the upper rooms of centuries of accumulated debris in 1934. Picks were carefully used to break up the hard-packed soil in preparation for being shoveled out. The gentleman at right in the photograph, just down the slope, is obviously a supervisor, as he holds no tool and a suit was not proper work attire.

Exposing and stabilizing the outside of the wall faces was a delicate and dangerous process on the steep side slopes of the ridge. One misstep could lead to a bad tumble and serious injury. There were no reports of such an incident during the entire project.

The 1934 crew is hard at work exposing the remains of the upper pueblo. Loose stones were removed and piled up to be used later in wall restoration work. Many stones not reused in that process were utilized in the construction of the museum that later became the Visitor Center.

The work crew is absent from this photograph of the same location. The pile of stones remains, indicating that the excavation of this area is not yet complete and the site has not been cleared of leftover building stones and other removed material.

This 1934 photograph shows the excavation crew, mostly unemployed copper workers from the surrounding towns. In the first row, second from left, in the dark shirt and hat, is Ben Lewis. It was his suggestion that gave the pueblo its name. At the opposite end of the first row, fourth and fifth from the end are Edward Spicer and Louis Caywood. While not all the men in this photograph are identified, some of the names noted include Serafin Herrea, Leo Vera, Bert Logan, Jack Hancock, Harry Getty, David Foulk, Roy Stacey, Juan Torre, Manuel Ballesfexos, Robert Parker, and Don Molins.

This photograph shows an exterior wall totally exposed, with the ground cleared and leveled at its base. The crew appears to have moved back to the top of the ridge to either excavate another wall section or dig down into the individual rooms.

A geometric pattern takes shape in this 1940 view down the south slope of the hill. This view has become an iconic image many photographers have duplicated over the intervening years. The installation of walkways above this section has enhanced the view.

This 1939 photograph was taken from the wetlands area to the southeast of Tuzigoot. Known as Tavasci Marsh, this area is fed by several underground springs and overflow waters from nearby Peck's Lake and the Verde River. During dry periods, however, it can be traversed on foot.

This photograph shows the northern section (units 1 and 3) of the top of Tuzigoot Hill from the vantage point of a restored roof, just prior to demolition of the room. The next 22 photographs are from a 1942 site survey report conducted by John L. Cotter, the first National Park Service director of Tuzigoot National Monument. Where unit and room numbers appear in photograph captions, please refer to the 1935 Caywood and Spicer map on page 28 for exact locations.

Seen here is a general view looking north at Unit 4. All existing features of the site were well-documented, as were any physical changes and improvements. This unit was totally reconstructed and then disassembled later when it began to deteriorate after only a few years.

This general view of Unit 4 is looking north. This unit was the northernmost portion of the pueblo and was separated from the rest of the complex by an open area. One possible reason for this usable building area being left open was for a communal work or meeting area.

This is an often photographed overview of Tuzigoot. Many more pictures would be taken by visitors in the years to come looking down from the top of the tower, or two-story, room of the pueblo in a southerly direction toward the Verde River and the present-day town of Cottonwood.

Unit 3, Room 7 (north wall) has a low remnant wall in this very small room. The small size of the room indicates it was a storage space rather than living quarters. In the background of the photograph are the remains of the reconstructed Unit 4, with a doorway that would never have existed in the original pueblo, before its final removal.

41

Pictured here is Unit 3, Room 9 (west wall). Had the Sinagua created windows and entry/exit doors in their rooms, this constant view of the valley below might have been impressive to them. One can only wonder if they admired this view, or just saw the land as something to be irrigated and planted with crops.

This photograph of Unit 4, Room 4 (second floor) is showing the reconstructed roof during its demolition. The concrete and wire netting top layer has already been removed, but some of the beams, cross poles, willow branches, and a layer of stone rubble still remain.

This view of Unit 5, Room 7 (north wall) shows the condition of the wall prior to the 1942 stabilization. Visitors, workmen, and family members were enlisted to be in the photographs to show size relation. Unfortunately, no names of those volunteers were recorded.

Duplication of photographs was rare, but this shot shows the same location as the previous one, only with a different little girl posing. This is also Unit 5, Room 7 (north wall), and the image shows the condition of the wall prior to stabilization.

This image of Unit 3, Room 6 (east wall) shows the condition of the wall. Unearthed metates and grinding stones, or manos, were lined up on display for this photograph prior to their removal for protection. Most of these items were put in safekeeping, with only a few returned to the rooms for use as visual aids.

Pictured is Unit 5, Room 8 (west wall). All repointing work shown here was done by the 1934 excavators except the north third, which is recent repointing work. Note that the copper smelter smokestack in the distance is still belching smoke in 1942, even though the copper industry was slowly shutting down at the time.

This image of the Unit 4 roof sections of Rooms 7, 5, and 3 was taken from the roof of Room 4, showing re-created rooftop entryways and ladders. Flickering electric lights were installed to simulate the glow of firepits when visitors looked into the darkened rooms. This entire reconstruction was later removed.

The east side of the reconstruction of the north Unit 4 is seen here. Note that the walls contained more fitted stones than the small original wall of irregularly shaped stones in the foreground. When the reconstructions became unstable and unsafe, they were eventually removed in 1942.

At Unit 5, Room 13 (south wall) recapping had been done by the 1934 excavators; the remainder of the wall is as it was originally uncovered. The buildings seen in upper right of the photograph are a chicken farm that once operated below Tuzigoot.

This is Unit 6, Room 7 (northwest corner) before any 1942 stabilization. In the background is the 1934 reconstruction of Unit 4, later removed, with uncharacteristic windows. Most of the south and east sides of the Visitor Center can also been seen from this angle.

Most of the north wall (Unit 5, Room 25) was repointed along the top and sides by the 1934 excavators. The west end, where the person is pointing, was repointed again by the inspection/maintenance crew in 1942, shortly before this photograph was taken.

The top of the south wall (Unit 5, Room 27) was reset by the 1934 excavators; the remainder of the wall is original. The tailings fields, where the by-product of the copper smelting process was dumped, were flooded periodically as a dust-control measure.

This overall picture of Unit 4 in 1942, in a view looking from the southeast to the northwest, shows the unit after the destruction and removal of the 1934 restored portions. A capping of restoration has been left on the wall tops above the original masonry.

An opposite angle of Unit 4 is shown in this view looking from southwest to the northeast after the destruction of the previously restored portions was completed. Visitor safety was a prime concern, and any unstable 1934 reconstruction was either removed or stabilized.

The walls all around this room, Unit 5, Room 23 (south wall), have been reset. The wall to the right of what appears to be three stone steps in the bottom left corner of the photograph has been stripped of the capping of flat stones placed there by the 1934 excavators.

Here, Unit 3 has a new retaining wall for the trail in the center foreground; the resurfacing of the path consisted of a bituminous mixture and crushed stone. The old trail surface and retaining wall had deteriorated badly through use and weathering.

This view of the reconstructed section of the second floor of Unit 4, Room 4 is showing the door in the south wall and part of the roof being removed. The reconstruction included walls of solid core concrete masonry two feet thick or more. The concrete had held moisture and blocked proper drainage, thus hastening deterioration.

In Unit 2, Room 1 (east wall), the top section was repointed by excavators in 1934. The bottom portion, below the barely visible rope on the wall in the foreground, was repointed in 1942. This photograph also shows a burial chamber in the process of being reopened and inspected in the background.

Seen here are before and after photographs from a 1953 restoration report. All work performed on the site was well-documented. The next 14 photographs are from that report. The first photograph (above) shows a low wall remnant displaying considerable erosion at its base, hastened by irregular stones that were poorly bedded and visitor use along the trail paralleling the wall. The second photograph (below) was taken after the wall was patched with soil cement. Where unit and room numbers appear in photograph captions, please refer to the 1935 Caywood and Spicer map on page 28 for the exact location.

The photograph above shows the northeast corner of a room that has worn away largely through unauthorized visitor entry into the room. The photograph below shows the view after the northeast corner was relaid and stabilized. Visitors making their own pathways in and out of the complex rooms has always been somewhat of a problem, but not one that cannot be dealt with.

Pictured above is the debris-filled southeast corner of Unit 4, Room 4, with modern rubble from dismantled restoration. The photograph below shows the room after the rubble has been removed. Found in the room were the charred stumps of modern upright poles in the floor; a rectangular, stone-lined fireplace in the center; and a clay-lined firepit in the corner—all in the same positions as their original locations, as that information was also uncovered.

These two photographs of the northeast corner of Unit 4, Room 4 show the area before (left) and after (below) the removal of the restoration debris. Once this was removed, future maintenance of the site became a much easier task to perform.

The northwest corner, in the angle formed by Room 6, a portion of which is visible at the extreme left, and Room 7, the wall at the right, are shown before the restoration debris removal (above) and after the debris was cleared (below).

The photograph at left shows a large quantity of restoration debris piled high inside unit 4, Room 6, looking to the northeast. Below, the room has been cleaned out. The difference between the two photographs is quite striking.

Two views of Unit 4, Room 7 (north wall) are pictured here. The photographs were taken before the debris was removed (above) and after the area was cleared and a previously installed water drain was repaired (below). Many other drains were installed throughout the complex but are cleverly disguised and unnoticeable.

In the above image, the clearing and removal of previous demolition debris north of Unit 4, Rooms 4 and 6, in 1953 is shown. As seen in the image below, the debris was loaded into trucks for easier transport away from the site for dumping or to other locations on-site to be reused.

Two photographs from a 1961 maintenance report are seen here. The east wall of Unit 4, Room 3 was loose and showed considerable uncolored concrete (right). This wall top was capped in tinted cement (below). Each phase of the work performed at the site was always well-documented. The next 20 photographs are from that report. Where unit and room numbers appear in photograph captions, please refer to the 1935 Caywood and Spicer map on page 28 for the exact location.

59

The south wall of Unit 4, Room 3 was recapped in order to obtain a more natural color (above). Further inspection of the wall revealed that no other repairs to the structure were needed, other than the recapping, at that time (below).

The west wall of Unit 4, Room 3 had been previously stabilized but was loose and crumbling (above). The wall was recapped using a tinted cement/mortar mixture to more closely simulate the mud used by the Sinagua (below).

Unit 4, Room 3 had been previously capped with a flat cement top (above). This was replaced with regular rough stone capping using a mud and concrete mixture to make it appear more authentic and original (below).

In Unit 4, Room 4 (north wall), the unauthentic, flat cement top of the wall was removed (above). The wall was then recapped with a tinted mud and concrete mixture to more closely resemble the original work (below).

Numerous small holes, probably caused by insects or rodents, had appeared in the east wall of Unit 4, Room 5 and were filled in (above). The wall was then recapped after stabilization (below).

The west wall of Unit 4, Room 5 was badly eroded, both on the top and on the wall face (above). Repointing and recapping were employed to stabilize the wall and prevent any further weather-related deterioration (below).

The south wall of Unit 4, Room 5 was loose and of odd-colored mortar, having been previously stabilized (above). The wall was securely capped, and the color was corrected with new mortar (below).

Numerous rodent holes and weathering are apparent in this photograph of the north wall of Unit 4, Room 6 (above). The holes were filled in, and the loose wall top was recapped for safety (below).

A large amount of rodent holes had created a dangerous situation in the exterior wall of Unit 4, Room 6 (above). Filling the holes and repointing minimized the danger of losing the wall to a collapse from weakness (below).

As evidenced in the above photograph, the old capping on Unit 4, Room 7 from 1942 was loose, unsightly, and dangerous. The south wall was recapped in correctly tinted mud and concrete mortar, as seen in the photograph below.

The above photograph is showing that much of the mortar in Unit 4, Room 7 had weathered away. This east wall was extensively repointed with tinted cement mortar, as shown in the follow-up photograph below.

In 1963, metal benches were added around the complex, like this one in front of Unit 4, Room 3. Visitors could now stop and rest during their walking tour of the site (sitting on the low wall tops is prohibited) and admire the surrounding Verde Valley landscape only minimally changed by the hand of man from years earlier when the 1934 excavation of the site began.

This 1965 photograph shows a maintenance worker applying new mortar to the south wall cap of Unit 4, Room 3. Due to continuous exposure to the elements, maintenance of the mortar, especially around the wall caps, is an ongoing task. In the past, a mixture of mud and concrete was used to replace crumbling concrete, and it continues to be used today. This mixture allows for better drainage and creates a more natural look more in keeping with the original plain mud mortar used by the Sinagua.

This photograph was taken on Memorial Day weekend in 1966. Saplings planted 30 years before, at the completion of the construction of the museum, later the Visitor Center, have now grown into full-height trees. Attendance has continued to increase since that time as more and more people find out about this hidden gem of a site. More than 100,000 visitors a year now pass through the gates to experience Tuzigoot.

These images were taken in 1968. Above are the north and west walls of Unit 4, Room 6 before they were grouted, capped, and refaced. Below shows the walls after the work was completed and the weeds were pulled out.

The 1968 maintenance/stabilization crew posed for this photograph outside the south end of the Visitor Center at the completion of their work. From left to right are (first row) Richard Jacquez, John Tavasci, archeologists Waggoner and Mayer, Lyman Lewis, and John Razo; (second row) Willie Yazzie, Paul Shorty, Ben Wilson, Jimmie Pablo, Jim Wero, Kee Johnson, and Lewis Napoleon. Wilson and Pablo appear to be holding a watermelon.

Accompanying these photographs from a 1992 maintenance report is a blunt and to-the-point caption. Referring to the east wall of Unit 4, Room 1, the page in the report is simply captioned with "Before capping" (left) and "After capping" (below). No other notations appear.

This view of the west side of Tuzigoot is looking up from the southwest. The photographer was standing near where a chicken farm was once located and on the flatlands where the copper smelting waste by-product, or tailings, was dumped for years before the copper mills closed down and the 2007 environmental cleanup and rehabilitation of the land took place. (Courtesy David Rose, www.arizonaruins.com.)

Sunrise at Tuzigoot is pictured here. The pueblo is an impressive sight in its natural setting and a fascinating photographic subject, no matter the season, time of day, or lighting conditions. This photograph was taken from a vantage point to the east and across the valley. (Courtesy David Rose, www.arizonaruins.com.)

This view is from the northeast side of the crest looking up at the 1934 re-created two-story structure known as the tower room. It is easy to see why early explorers of the Southwest thought pueblos such as Tuzigoot were fortresses. The thick walls lacked any exterior doors or windows. (Courtesy David Rose, www.arizonaruins.com.)

This view is looking south toward the town of Cottonwood from the top of the two-story tower room structure. Note that the smokestack visible in photographs from previous years is now gone, having been torn down after the copper mill closed. (Courtesy David Rose, www.arizonaruins.com.)

This view is looking north up toward the southern slope of Tuzigoot from the flatlands below. Native vegetation now obscures the view of the south slope portion of the complex from this angle. (Courtesy David Rose, www.arizonaruins.com.)

This doorway into the re-created two-story dwelling, or tower room, was designed to facilitate visitor entry in 1934. All of the entryways in the original pueblo were through the roofs with the use of ladders. This re-creation was erected to showcase the interior construction of the structure and needed ease of visitor entry to do so. (Courtesy David Rose, www.arizonaruins.com.)

This photograph shows the doorway of the re-created two-story room seen from the metal stairway to the roof of the building. Once on top, the visitor has an unobstructed view of the entire pueblo and of the surrounding Verde Valley in any direction. It is the only 1934 re-creation that remains today; the others were removed. (Author's collection.)

The entire complex is pictured here from the east side of the valley. The southern section of the pueblo snakes down the slope at left, and the Visitor Center is at right and separate from the pueblo. It is not hard to imagine what this complex must have looked like with its roofs intact and people moving about the buildings so long ago. (Courtesy David Rose, www.arizonaruins.com.)

The museum/Visitor Center was completed in the 1930s. While the Tuzigoot complex has remained virtually unchanged from its original 1934 excavation and restoration, the Visitor Center has undergone many upgrades over the years.

The landscaped Visitor Center is pictured here in 2016. Currently, it is a shady haven for visitors after their walking tour of the pueblo grounds and perhaps before they peruse the souvenir section inside. (Courtesy Barbara Prichard.)

The open and airy interior of the Visitor Center retains the original artifacts excavated at the site. They are on display in roughly the same area, after some slight rearranging, that the previous 1934 museum once showed them in. Today, there is also a small souvenir and book area, and the staff is happy to help the customer find just the right memento of his or her visit. (Courtesy David Rose, www.arizonaruins.com.)

While the Tuzigoot pueblo appears unchanged over the years since its final configuration was created in 1942 with the removal of most of the 1934 failing reconstructions, maintenance efforts are constantly under way. In this photograph, a 1992 work crew recaps a wall in Unit 4, Room 1. Regular site inspection and scheduled maintenance keep the pueblo in the best condition possible.

A 2013 maintenance crew, visible just above left center on the south walking path, works on one of the southern slope rooms covered with a protective tarp. A workman pushing a wheelbarrow used to mix mud and concrete is seen in front of the tarp. This photograph was taken from the rooftop of the tower room. Today, a two-man maintenance crew oversees the site full-time, and extra workmen are hired depending on the size and scope of the project undertaken. (Courtesy Barbara Prichard.)

In 2016, the two-story central structure known as the tower room underwent stabilization maintenance. The tower room is the only 1934 reconstruction that was judged safe enough to remain standing during the 1942 inspection of the site. The exterior of the re-created structure was so tall, this maintenance crew had to work on scaffolding. This view is looking up from the west walking path. (Courtesy Barbara Prichard.)

These views looking up toward the tower room from the paved walking trail along the base of the walls show the west side of the Tuzigoot summit in 2016. Together, the two images create an almost complete close-up of the entire side. (Both, courtesy Barbara Prichard.)

These views looking up toward the tower room from the paved walking trail along the base of the walls show the east side of the Tuzigoot summit in 2016. As on page 87, the two images together create an almost complete close-up of the entire side. (Both, courtesy Barbara Prichard.)

With a view looking down at the southeastern slope dwellings, this photograph was taken from the paved walking trail on the east side of Tuzigoot. A residential area of the town of Cottonwood is visible in the distance. Tuzigoot is surrounded by almost 50 acres of protected lowlands, so the chances of private dwellings coming any closer than where they are now located are nonexistent. (Courtesy Barbara Prichard.)

This view from the south side walking trail is looking up toward the summit tower room. More photographs have probably been taken from the tower room rooftop than from any other location in the entire complex. (Courtesy Barbara Prichard.)

This view looking north toward the Visitor Center is from the top of the two-story tower room. The view was once obstructed by the reconstructed Unit 4, since removed, as seen in earlier photographs taken from the same vantage point. (Courtesy Barbara Prichard.)

In this view looking south at Tuzigoot from the north, the Visitor Center in the foreground. One can stand here and wonder what Tuzigoot might have looked like had the Sinagua not abandoned the site but had continued to build along this lower portion of the ridge to this point. The mountains in the background have a light covering of snow on them in this 2013 photograph. (Courtesy Barbara Prichard.)

This photograph was taken from the northern end of the paved nature trail with a view looking south toward the Visitor Center in the foreground and Tuzigoot pueblo in the background. Along this nature trail, there are many informational signs describing the local plants that can be seen there. (Courtesy Barbara Prichard.)

The lush Verde Valley is viewed from the southern paved walking trail of Tuzigoot. This trail is just below the southern ridge summit and above the south slope complex of rooms. (Courtesy Barbara Prichard.)

The life-sustaining Verde River continues to ebb and flow below Tuzigoot, as it has done for eons. The water once nourished crops planted by the Sinagua and allowed the people to remain here comfortably for centuries before they mysteriously left. (Courtesy Barbara Prichard.)

This first aerial photograph of the east side of Tuzigoot appears in the 1935 report *Tuzigoot: The Excavation and Repair of a Ruin on the Verde River near Clarkdale, Arizona*, by Louis R. Caywood and Edward H. Spicer. It was printed by the National Park Service Field Division of Education.

Another aerial photograph from the late 1940s is seen here. It was taken to show the proximity of fields of dumped tailings from the copper ore refining process at nearby smelters. The fields contaminated with that waste are visible in the upper and left center in this view looking westward from above.

This serene scene of a snow-covered Tuzigoot was taken in 2016, the year the National Park Service celebrated its 100th birthday. For 77 of those years, the National Park Service has administered, preserved, and maintained the site for generations of visitors to marvel at and enjoy. Recent psychological studies indicate that exposure to the natural environment fosters improved mental health, and this is the perfect place to engage in that sort of contact. (Courtesy Critical Eye Photography and Doug Von Gausig.)

BIBLIOGRAPHY

Adler, Michael A., ed. *The Prehistoric Pueblo World A.D. 1150–1350.* Tucson: University of Arizona Press, 1996.

Caywood, Louis R., and Edward H. Spicer. *Tuzigoot: The Excavation and Repair of a Ruin on the Verde River near Clarkdale, Arizona.* Berkeley, CA: US Department of the Interior National Park Service Field Division of Education, 1935.

Houk, Rose. *Sinagua, Prehistoric Cultures of the Southwest.* Tucson: Western National Parks Association, 1992.

———. *Tuzigoot National Monument.* Tucson: Western National Parks Association, 1995.

Protas, Josh. *A Past Preserved in Stone: A History of Montezuma Castle National Monument.* Tucson: Western National Parks Association, 2002.

Discover Thousands of Local History Books Featuring Millions of Vintage Images

Arcadia Publishing, the leading local history publisher in the United States, is committed to making history accessible and meaningful through publishing books that celebrate and preserve the heritage of America's people and places.

Find more books like this at
www.arcadiapublishing.com

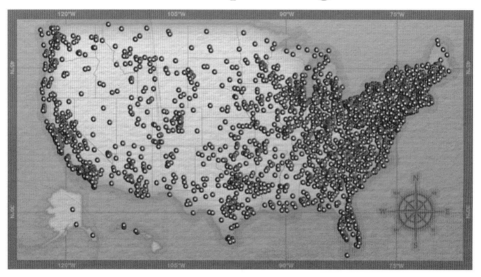

Search for your hometown history, your old stomping grounds, and even your favorite sports team.

Consistent with our mission to preserve history on a local level, this book was printed in South Carolina on American-made paper and manufactured entirely in the United States. Products carrying the accredited Forest Stewardship Council (FSC) label are printed on 100 percent FSC-certified paper.